A Bug in a Jug
and Other Funny Rhymes

written by Gloria Patrick
illustrated by Alan Baker

D.C. Heath and Company
HEATH Lexington, Massachusetts / Toronto, Ontario

Acknowledgments

Grateful acknowledgment is made for permission to reprint the following copyrighted material.

A BUG IN A JUG AND OTHER FUNNY RHYMES, by Gloria Patrick. Copyright © 1970 by Carolrhoda Books, Inc., 241 First Avenue North, Minneapolis, Minnesota, 55401. Reprinted by permission of the publisher.

Design   Brown Publishing Network, Inc.

Copyright © 1993 by D. C. Heath and Company

All rights reserved. No part of this publication may be reproduced or transmitted in any form by any means, electronic or mechanical, including photocopy, recording, or any information storage or retrieval system, without permission in writing from the publisher.

Printed simultaneously in Canada

Printed in the United States of America

International Standard Book Number: 0-669-30229-5

2 3 4 5 6 7 8 9 10-POO-96 95 94 93

This is a mouse.

This is a house.

This is the mouse in the house.

T his is a louse.

T his is the louse
on the mouse
in the house.

This is a jug.

This is a rug.

This is the jug on the rug.

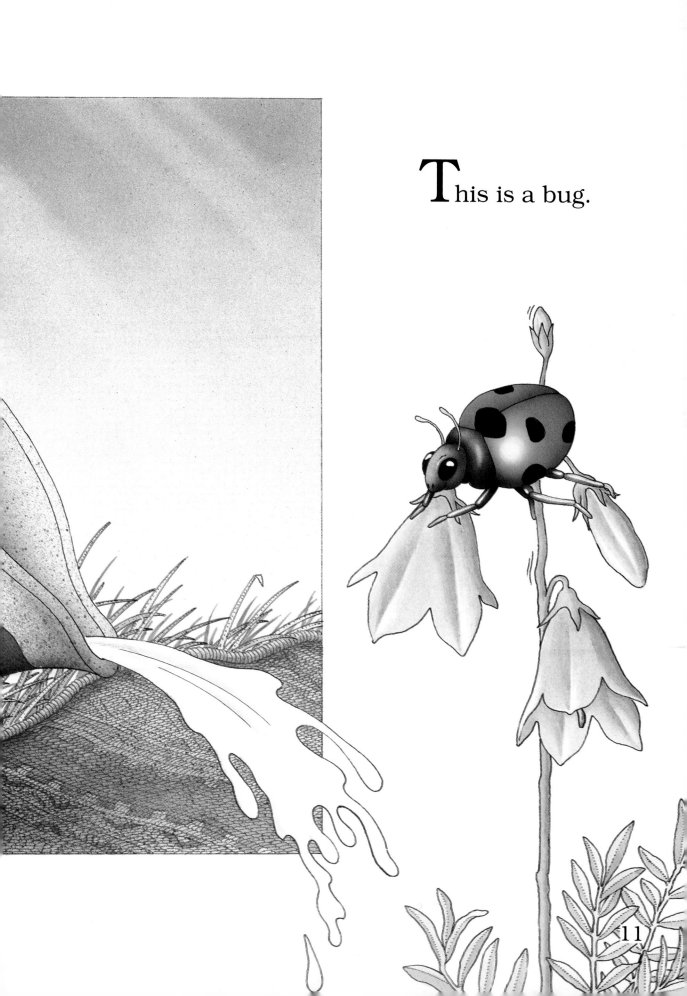

This is a bug.

11

This is a bug
in the jug
on the rug.

This is a cat.

This is a hat.

14

Τhis is the cat in the hat.

This is a mat.

This is the cat
in the hat
on the mat.

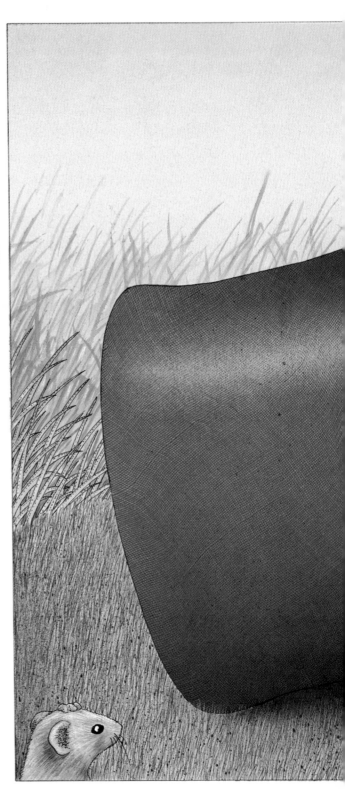

This is a bee.

This is me.

This is the bee chasing me.

This is a tree.

This is the bee
chasing me
up the tree.

20

This is a dog.

This is a log.

This is the dog on the log.

This is the fog.

This is the dog
on the log
in the fog.

This is my friend.

This is a bend.

This is my friend at the bend.

This is the end.

A Bug in a Jug

and Other Funny Rhymes

This is a mouse.
This is a house.
This is the mouse in the house.
This is a louse.
This is the louse
    on the mouse
    in the house.

This is a jug.
This is a rug.
This is the jug on the rug.
This is a bug.
This is a bug
    in the jug
    on the rug.

This is a cat.
This is a hat.
This is the cat in the hat.
This is a mat.
This is the cat
    in the hat
    on the mat.

This is a bee.
This is me.
This is the bee chasing me.
This is a tree.
This is the bee
    chasing me
    up the tree.

This is a dog.
This is a log.
This is the dog on the log.
This is the fog.
This is the dog
    on the log
    in the fog.

This is my friend.
This is a bend.
This is my friend at the bend.
This is the end.